LeGEND

 INTRODUCING THE TOPIC   DISCUSSING WITH THE GROUP

 EXPLORING CREATIVELY   STUDYING THE SCRIPTURE

 STORYTELLING   REFLECTION

 ROLEPLAY   SMALL GROUP OR PAIRED DISCUSSION

Dedicated to the memory of Lanny Chandler, whose enthusiasm, humor and faith inspired a generation of young people.

Living the Good News, Inc.
a division of Church Publishing Incorporated
Editorial Offices
600 Grant Street, Suite 400
Denver, CO 80203

Cover Design and Layout: Val Price
Photography: Marc Dickey, Regan MacStravic, Ann Addison

Printed in the United States of America.

The scripture-based activities contained herein have been created using the Today's English Version, © 1992, American Bible Society. Used by permission.

ISBN 978-1889108-07-0
ISBN 1-889108-07-3

Quick Takes for teens

Easy, on-the-spot Resources for Youth ministry

volume 3

World PROBLEMS

Dirk deVries

INTRoDUCTiON

For me it started in Denver in the early 1980's. I was — finally — a youth pastor! A teen beacon, a shepherd to the oddly-shorn sheep, a hip-hop, happenin', cool guide through the rocky crags of adolescence into the grateful, fruitful plains of adulthood. It was my calling, my mission, my vision.

"Didn't you know," someone cheerfully asked, "that the average youth pastor only lasts eighteen months?" *Eighteen months?* What kind of legacy can I leave in eighteen months? I expected to be doing this at least along enough to receive two generations' worth of nice thank-you notes.

But no, according to the stats — back then anyway — most of us could only stand eighteen months of...

- sleepless weekend retreats where — due to either a planning glitch or our own innocent inexperience — we not only led all the sessions, all the games and all the rites, but also stayed awake all night saying "Quiet down!" "Get back in your room!" and "I mean it this time!"
- pacifying the custodian who demanded to know who stuck the pizza (pepperoni and mushroom) to the ceiling of the fellowship hall
- listening to the teen who just...got dumped by his girlfriend...learned her parents are divorcing...got rejected from the college she'd dreamed of attending...lost his place on the soccer team

I lasted five and a half years, proud, I might point out, to have gone four years beyond the average. But I couldn't really give it up; there's something that gets under your skin...or under mine, anyway. And if you are reading this book, you share this desire to make God's grace real for teens. Whether full-time or for ninety minutes a week, you are a "youth minister."

And you are very busy.

And so we designed this book for you.

No, not more session plans. Just tons of proven, practical, creative activities from which to pick and choose...

- to fill in an already prepared but incomplete meeting
- to supplement a catechetical session when some topic demands immediate attention
- to open or close a meeting
- to fill an extra 15-20 minutes you didn't expect to have

It's a wild smorgasbord of opportunities for your group.

This book also acknowledges that no two groups are the same. Your group is unique. No other group faces the same mix of issues, with the same time constraints, the same interests and the same abilities. An a la carte menu of possibilities makes

(continued on next page)

4

sense — prayers, discussions starters, art, drama and music choices. You choose what your experience and intuition tell you will work the best.

I encourage you to browse through the book before the need for it arises. Get a feel for the broad topic areas so that, when you need an activity or a discussion starter, you'll already know where to look and what's available. Flag ideas that strike you as particularly useful for your group.

Bolded words key you in immediately to needed materials or required preparation. Easy-to-find symbols throughout the book help fit activity styles to your needs.

LeGEND

 INTRODUCING THE TOPIC   DISCUSSING WITH THE GROUP

 EXPLORING CREATIVELY   STUDYING THE SCRIPTURE

 STORYTELLING   REFLECTION

 RULEPLAY    SMALL GROUP OR PAIRED DISCUSSION

ToPiCS

Here's a quick run-down of the topics in this volume of Quick Takes:

- *Global Concerns:* This section explores four topics with particular world impact: HIV and AIDS, natural disasters, the environment and refugees. You'll find a variety of creative ways to examine these problems, including how to identify our own responsibility in relieving the suffering they bring.

- *Media Mania:* Here you'll find ways to start discussions about television, films, video games, music videos and magazines. Group members will be encouraged to become media savvy, watching and listening with discernment, and to resist the subtle influences of advertising and the pressures of today's media hype.

- *Poverty and Wealth:* In this section, activities offer ways to help teens identify and combat the dangers of materialism, commercialism and consumerism. Participants can also explore a number of topics related to issues of poverty and wealth, including homelessness, gambling and hunger. Finally, several activities take a broader look at life-goals and values, encouraging group members to make wise choices when it comes to their time, energy and money.

- *Violence:* This portion of the book offers suggestions for helping group members articulate their experiences, fears, feelings and thoughts about a variety of violence-related topics, including family violence, bullying, child abuse, sexual abuse, TV violence, war, guns, murder and capital punishment.

We hope you have fun and find meaning with the members of your group using the ideas presented in Quick Takes, Volume 3.

TiPS

- Pray. Begin and end your preparation with prayer. Leading youth is an awesome opportunity *and* responsibility. Prepare well; surrender control to God.
- Listen. Then listen some more. Then listen even more. Don't preach. Don't be an expert. Share from your experience with the humble knowledge that only by the grace of God will it have relevance.
- Know yourself. Practice attending to your feelings, your thoughts, your desires, your fears, your hurts, your confusion at any given moment. Be willing to acknowledge your honest self, warts and all. Kids respond to—and model—this kind of Christlike transparency.
- Practice vulnerability. Would you share your heart with someone who seemed unable or unwilling to share theirs?
- Discipline consistently. State group rules clearly, along with the consequences for breaking them. Follow through for infractions. Apply the same rules and consequences for all kids. The group will appreciate not only knowing the limits, but being able to trust them.
- Adolescence is a turbulent, topsy-turvy time. Expect sudden emotional swings— from energy to apathy—and seemingly inappropriate responses. As kids mature, rational discussion replaces these surprising outbursts of tears or frustration.
- Kids want to be perfect—physically, academically, socially, emotionally. Help them see that imperfection and failure are a part of being human and very much okay. Good-naturedly acknowledging and accepting your *own* imperfection is a good place to start.

ICeBReAKeRS
WHeRE i AM, WHeRE i'M NoT

Circle the group, inviting each member to quickly tell the group:
- where they would rather be at the moment
- where they are glad they're *not* at the moment

SoNG ReWRiTE

Instruct group members to turn to the 2-3 people nearest them. Ask each of these small groups to quickly rewrite the words to a popular children's song so that they say something about "welcoming each other" (or any other topic relevant to the meeting's focus). Encourage good humor.

Here is an example, sung to the tune of "Twinkle, Twinkle Little Star":

> Welcome, welcome each of you
> To our strange yet cordial group.
> We hope that you stick around.
> Friendship here is to be found.
> Welcome, welcome each of you
> To our strange yet cordial group.

Ask groups to sing their new songs to the other groups.

IF I CoULD...

Distribute an **index card** and **pencil** to each group member. Explain:

- On your card, answer these three questions:
    - If I was given $500 right now, and I had to spend it in the next hour, what would I buy?
    - If I could effortlessly change one thing about my home, what would it be?
    - If I could meet any person in history, living or dead, who would it be?

When group members have finished, collect their cards and invite each member to introduce him- or herself.

After introductions, mix the cards. Choose one card and read one answer from it. Invite members to discuss whose card it might be. Let the group *collectively* make one guess as to the identity of the card's owner. If they are incorrect, read the next answer on the card and let the group once again discuss and guess. Read the third answer if the group is still incorrect. If the group fails to correctly guess the author of the card, return the card to the stack and repeat the process with another guess. If the author of the card is correctly guessed, remove the card from the stack.

Continue until all members have been correctly linked to their cards.

NaME TaGS

You can base a number of creative ice breakers on the creation of name tags. Here are a few suggestions:

- Have group members create their own name tags using **a variety of materials**: construction paper, scissors, glue, ribbon, gummed stars, stickers, pipe cleaners, cereal pieces, string, yarn, macaroni, etc.
- Invite group members to add not only their names to their tags, but also symbols representing one or more interests. Have members guess the meaning of the symbols.
- Have group members make "animal name tags," each member picturing an animal that best represents his or her personality. Let members explain their choices to the group. The same method an used for creating "food name tags," "plant name tags" or "car name tags."
- Group members make name tags for each other, following any of the methods mentioned above.

Global Concerns

GLOBAL CONCERNS

AiDS GRaFFiTi

Post several **sheets of news-print** around the room. Then divide into small groups, one per sheet. Distribute **markers** to each group and invite members to cover their sheets with comments, reactions, feelings or ideas about AIDS. Ask members not to censor one another's graffiti at this point. Continue with the activity AIDS Accounts on page 11.

AiDiNG OuTCaSTS

Distribute **Bibles** and ask one group member to read aloud Leviticus 13:1-8, 45-46. Ask:

■ How were people with skin diseases treated in biblical times? What similarities or differences do you see between this treatment and how people with AIDS are treated today?

Then ask another group member to read aloud Mark 1:40-42. Ask:

■ How does Jesus treat the man with the skin disease? How do his action and attitude compare to the description from Leviticus?

■ Some people have suggested that AIDS is God's punishment for immoral behavior, like sexual promiscuity or drug abuse. Do you agree or disagree? Why?

■ Jesus touched the man with the skin disease. How would he treat someone dying of AIDS today? What do you think he would say to us about the way we treat people with AIDS?

AN ENViRoNMeNTaL THiNG

Post a sheet of **newsprint** to the wall. Title it The Environment. Ask a volunteer to record group members' responses as they brainstorm a list of their environmental concerns. After 5 minutes of brainstorming, stop and ask the group to choose their top five concerns. Divide into five groups, each taking the concern that its members find most compelling. Ask each group to come up with the name of an organization that will address this concern and its primary method of action (e.g., lobbying, protesting, demonstrations, fundraising, etc.). After several minutes, ask groups to share their work.

NaTURaL DiSASTeRS: HeLP!

Distribute **a variety of recent newspapers and news magazines**. Ask group members to find and report on natural disasters around the globe, including floods, fires, disease, drought, etc. Ask them to assess the depth of suffering and the effectiveness of relief efforts.

GOD'S WoRLD, OuR WoRLD

Sit in a circle and together compose a simple prayer litany. Go around the circle, letting each group member offer a one-sentence prayer for some global concern. After each group member has prayed, the group can respond in unison with: *God's world, our world*.

GOD aND THe ENViRoNMeNT

Distribute **Bibles** and divide the group into small groups of three or four members. Give each group **paper** and **a pencil** with these instructions: Read Psalm 8 together and then rewrite it in contemporary language.

When groups have finished, let a volunteer from each group read the group's rewrite. Then ask:

- ■ What does it mean to be "appointed a ruler" over everything God has made?
- ■ How do you think God feels about how humanity has cared for the earth?
- ■ What attitudes and beliefs cause environmental problems?
- ■ What attitudes and beliefs does this psalm mention that would lead to environmental health?

ENViRoNMeNTaL ADDReSS

Distribute **paper, pens, envelopes** and **stamps**. Post a sheet with the **names** and **addresses** of local, state or national politicians (city council members, senators, representatives). Divide into small groups and ask each group to choose one environmental concern its members share and to write a group letter to one of the politicians. The letter should express their concern and either suggest an alternative way of dealing with the issue or support the way it is now handled.

AiDS ACCoUNTS

Begin with the activity AIDS Graffiti (p. 8). Then give these instructions: Give each member of your group 2 minutes to respond to your graffiti and to tell how the AIDS epidemic has affected him or her personally. (Stories could include feelings or impressions about AIDS, accounts of friends with AIDS, etc.)

AcTS OF GoD

Distribute **Bibles** and divide into groups of three or four. Assign each group one of the following scripture readings that illustrate God's care for God's people during natural disasters:

- Drought: 1 Kings 17:1-16
- Flood: Genesis 6—8
- Famine: Psalm 33:18-19; 37:18-19
- Storms at Sea: Acts 27:13-44

Ask each group to read its assigned passage and to prepare a brief summary of the reading for the other groups. In addition, ask each group to discuss its reading:

- What disaster takes place in this reading?
- How does God intervene to spare the lives of God's people in this reading?

When groups are ready, regather and ask representatives from each group to summarize both the readings and the group discussions.

AiDiNG PEoPLE WiTH AiDS

Before your meeting contact your local health department for current information on AIDS and AIDS prevention; they may have pamphlets to distribute. The National AIDS Information Hotline is 1-800-342-AIDS. Share AIDS information with group members and discuss:

- Do you know someone with AIDS? What has your relationship with this person taught you about AIDS? about life? about death?
- How aware of AIDS are the students in your school? How seriously do those at risk take the warnings about AIDS?
- What would happen in your family if you were diagnosed with AIDS? in your school? in your church? with your friends?
- What special needs do those with AIDS face? In what ways can we meet those needs?

FIVE AIDS FACTS

#1 AIDS is caused by a virus called HIV, which stands for *human immunodeficiency virus.* AIDS stands for *Acquired Immunodeficiency Syndrome.* HIV attacks the person's immune system, weakening it until it can no longer resist other diseases.

#2 Anyone can get HIV. Sexually active straight teenagers are the fastest-growing segment of AIDS cases in the U.S. Most people with HIV or AIDS get the virus by having sex or sharing needles with someone who is already infected. Pregnant women can spread the virus to their babies during pregnancy or childbirth.

#3 You cannot "catch" HIV like a cold or the flu. It is not spread through the air, through water or through casual contact.

#4 It may take many years for people who are infected with HIV to develop AIDS. Until then, they may look and feel fine but they can still infect others. It is estimated that between 1-1.5 million Americans have been infected with the virus by the early 1990s but have not yet developed clinical symptoms.

#5 Right now, there is no cure for AIDS. However, you can protect yourself from the virus. Do not have sex. Condoms provide some protection from infection, but they are not completely effective. You can still get HIV even if you use a condom. Do not use drugs. Sharing a needle with someone who has HIV can get you infected. Even if you do not *shoot* drugs, drug use can cause you to make other foolish and life-threatening decisions that can lead to AIDS.

ReFUGee EMoTIonS

Begin with the activity Refugee Night (p. 15). Then invite group members to discuss the situation, using these or similar questions:

- How does it feel to be a refugee?
- Imagine that you are in a country where English is not spoken. How will you go about applying for a job? finding other housing? signing up for school? getting food for your friends and family? communicating with the people you left behind?
- How will you cope with the loss of your home, friends, family, school, job, town, clothing, tapes and CDS, bike, computer — all the things with which you were familiar and with which you filled your life?
- What will you miss most about your old life?
- What do you think will be the biggest hurdle to overcome in establishing a new life?
- What part do you expect God to play in your new life as a refugee?

AiDS: SURPRiSeD?

Begin with the activity AIDS Graffiti (p. 8). Then review Five AIDS Facts with the group (p. 12). After each fact, ask:

- Is this new information to anyone?
- Does this fact surprise you? disturb you? puzzle you? reassure you?

Ask participants to return to their groups that composed the graffiti. Give these instructions: Circle those words, phrases or ideas that you would like to change or discuss. Talk together about how your impressions about AIDS have changed.

Global Concerns

13

THe ExiLED

Distribute **Bibles** and invite group members to turn together to Psalms 42 and 43.

Explain:

- For part of their history, the Jewish people were exiled from their Palestinian homeland and carried off to live for 70 years in the foreign country of Babylon. These were dark days for the Jewish refugees. Psalms 42 and 43 reflect this experience.

Read Psalms 42 and 43. Discuss:

- What different feelings does the psalmist experience?
- What does the psalmist hope for?
- How does the psalmist feel about God?
- What does the psalmist ask of God?
- To what extent do you think these psalms reflect the experience of today's refugees?
- Who *are* today's refugees? Who are the refugees in our community? our country? our world? (Review the information provided in Refugee Realities in the next column.)
- What special challenges do refugees face? What barriers do they face, which most of us do not?
- What can Christians do to help refugees here in our community? in our country? around the world?

REFUGEE REALITIES

- Refugees are people forced to leave their country by war, persecution, racism, natural disaster or economics. Most face life without the security, status or comfort they left behind.
- Worldwide, there have been tens of millions of refugees since 1901, the start of the century, causing some historians to label the 20th century the "age of the refugee."
- Wars result in refugees. The Viet Nam War produced over 2 million refugees. The Soviet invasion of Afghanistan in 1979 turned 6 million people into refugees. The Korean War caused 9 million people to flee their homes for asylum in other countries.
- Experts estimate that by 1991 16 million people were refugees around the world.
- Canada, Australia and the United States have traditionally welcomed the greatest number of the world's refugees. Increased competition for jobs and economic resources have caused many countries to question or limit their refugee policies. Some, like Switzerland and Japan, either forbid asylum for refugees or limit immigration of any type.

CLiPS oF CRisiS

In the last several decades, many popular films have graphically illustrated disasters such as earthquakes, fires, tornadoes, floods, epidemics and plane crashes. Typically, such films not only depict the fearsome power of disasters, but also a wide variety of human responses.

Illustrate the frightening nature and awesome power of disasters (both natural and of human origin) by showing **excerpts from one or more disaster-movie videos.** View an entire film on one disaster, or select two or three such movies and view their most exciting sequences.

After viewing each video, discuss:

■ How realistically do you think this film depicts the disaster? people's responses to the disaster?

■ With which character did you most identify? How do you think you would respond in the situation depicted in the film?

■ To what extent was God or faith in God acknowledged in this film?

■ If you had produced or directed this film, what would you have done differently?

ReFUGee NiGHt

Gather group members for what appears to be a regular meeting. Interrupt the beginning of the meeting to announce something like this:

■ Our city has been invaded by an unknown military group.

■ We are being driven out, forced to leave without the opportunity to talk to our families or friends, without going home to get our clothing or favorite possessions.

■ We are refugees.

Load group members into vehicles and travel to a nearby home. Give each group member a **blanket** and **a pillow**. Make available a **bag of old, used clothes**. Crowd group members together into a relatively small space — a dark basement would be ideal — and explain:

■ This is your new home. This room is where you will sleep and eat as you adjust to your new surroundings.

■ You have only the clothes on your back, plus what you share from this bag of old, donated clothing.

Extend the simulation as resources allow. You could, for example, serve a "meal" of **rice, beans** and **water**.

Follow this activity with Refugee Emotions on page 13.

Media Mania

GLuTToNY OR ENTeRTAiNMeNT?

Before the meeting invite several group members each to prepare a **videotape** of several minutes of what they consider to be entertaining television programming. Ask members not to bring anything potentially offensive due to language, sex or violence.

In addition, gather **examples of entertainment options** available to group members, either actual items (for example, a concert ticket, a novel, a CD, a teen-oriented magazine, a video game cartridge, etc.) or pictures of items or activities (a photo of an amusement park ride, a motorcycle, a home theater setup, etc.).

Together look through the items and pictures. Discuss:
- Which of these do you find most entertaining?
- In your opinion, what makes an item or activity "entertaining"? To be really entertaining, what must it include?

View the videos prepared **before the meeting**. Discuss:
- Of the examples of television entertainment we are viewing, which do you find most entertaining?
- When it comes to television, what makes a program "entertaining" for you? What must it include?
- Some have said we live in a culture "addicted" to entertainment. Do you agree? disagree?
- Define the term *entertainment addiction*.
- What would entertainment addiction look like if you saw it in a friend? in yourself?
- What is it about entertainment that makes it seem addictive? Why, for example, do we find the need to have scary entertainment get scarier? violent entertainment get more violent? sexy entertainment get sexier?

TV SuRVeY

Distribute **paper** and **pencils** and invite group members to jot down answers to these questions:

- How many hours of TV do you think the average American watches a day?
- How many hours of TV do you think the average American teenager watches a day?
- On average, how many hours of TV do you watch each day?
- What type of shows do you most like to watch?
- What type of shows do you least like?
- During what percentage of your TV watching time do you simultaneously do other things like homework, hobbies or chores?
- Why do you watch TV? Choose from the following:
  - a) to fill empty time
  - b) to stay informed
  - c) to watch certain shows
  - d) to escape reality
  - e) to laugh
  - f) other (describe)

TV ReSULTS

Begin with the activity TV Survey. When group members have finished, tabulate the results, question by question, on **chalkboard or newsprint**. Share Television Trivia below with the group.

Ask:

- Which of these statistics surprised you?
- What new insight do you gain about television from these statistics?

TELEVISION TRIVIA

FACT The average American adult watches about 4 hours of TV a day.

FACT The average American teenager watches about 3 hours of TV every day.

FACT During the first 18 years of life, most children spend more time watching TV than going to school.

FACT In a lifetime, the average American spends over 95,000 hours watching TV.

FACT 20% of your TV watching time is spent watching ads.

FACT Prime-time TV features about five violent acts per hour; cartoons feature 20! Between kindergarten and 8th grade, the average child sees more than 13,000 murders on television.

TV: GeT A LiFE!

Distribute **Bibles, pencils** and **paper** and divide participants into three groups. Assign each a group a different portion of Colossians 3:1-17: verses 1-4, verses 5-11 and verses 12-17. Give these instructions: In your group, read your assigned portion of Colossians 3. When you've finished reading, summarize in one or two sentences what you believe is the main point of your group's passage.

After groups have finished their reading and summarizing, invite a representative from each group to share results. Then give these instructions: Now write a statement applying your understanding of Colossians 3 to the topic of television. What do you think Paul—the writer of the letter—would want us to understand about television if he were around today to see its influence?

Regather and ask the representatives from the groups to read their statements. Then ask:

- What do you think are "the things of heaven" (v. 1)? Why does Paul want us to focus on such things?
- According to verses 12-13, we are to "clothe ourselves" with compassion, kindness, humility, gentleness, patience, tolerance and forgiveness. How could we use television to help us do this?

18

MY THiNKiNG

Place a chair in the center of the circle. Invite volunteers to come one at a time to sit in the chair and finish these sentences:

- Television relieves my stress by...
- Television creates stress for me by...
- If I gave up one hour of television a week, I would...
- If I gave up one hour of television a day, I would...
- I usually watch television instead of...

TeLeViSiON MeSMeRiSM

Before your meeting, prepare a **video sampler** of 10 minutes of television: a commercial, parts of a music video, a segment of a sitcom or soap opera, etc. Set up a **TV** and **VCR** in your meeting room.

After watching each segment, stop the tape and critique what you are watching using these questions:

- What were the producers of this little chunk of TV trying to say to us? What do they want us to believe? to feel? to think? to buy?
- Do we agree with the message? Why or why not?
- How do you think God feels about this message?
- What kind of television programming do you think God would produce?

TV: HoW MuCH iS TOo MuCH?

Ask each group member to reflect on his or her own television-viewing habits. Use these questions as needed:

- Why do you watch TV?
- Do you think you watch too much TV? just the right amount?
- How would you know if you were watching too much TV? What would be the "symptoms"?
- How has TV influenced you for good or bad?
- If, for whatever reason, you could no longer watch TV, what would you do instead?
- How does TV influence our families? How would our families be different without television?
- How do you imagine TV has changed our relationships? our schools? our churches?

Then give each group member who wishes three minutes to tell the story of his or her TV experiences. Suggest that they speak in third-person, as though telling the story of someone they have observed. (*Example:* I know this girl named Kayla. She watches...) After each person has spoken, invite comments from the other group members. Comments should also be kept in the third person. (*Example:* Kayla seems to be hiding behind the TV. I think she...)

CeNSoRSHiP: YeS oR No?

Before your meeting put a **magazine** inside of a **paper bag** and seal it shut.

Display the paper bag. Divide into two groups, labeled FOR and AGAINST. Explain:

- Within this bag is a magazine that contains sexually explicit pictures, some involving children.
- The FOR group must defend the magazine, giving reasons why censorship of such materials is wrong.
- The AGAINST group must explain why the magazine should be banned.

Let the groups alternate statements for and against censorship of the magazine. After several minutes of debate, discuss:

- What pros and cons of censorship are we discovering in our debate?
- When might censorship be right in some situations and wrong in others?
- In cases like this, who decides what is to be censored? What criteria do we use?

Repeat the activity using the same bag but describing alternative contents. Examples:

- The bag contains a book by an author who believes that a certain ethnic group is inferior and should be refused civil rights.
- The bag contains a book that describes ways to commit suicide.
- The bag contains a magazine that explains to young people how to have safe sex.

THE GREaTeST MoViE EVeR MaDE

Distribute **paper** and **pencils**. Divide participants into smaller groups of 3-4 members each and give these instructions: With your small group, plan a 5-minute movie to be shown at halftime during the next Super Bowl. Your plan should address these questions: What will it be about? How will you make it the most authentically entertaining movie ever made? What's the plot? Who will star in it? What kind of special effects will it have? How will you hold people's attention? After the movie, how will people feel? How will they be changed?

After about 10 minutes, regather and ask volunteers from each group to share their plans for their movies. Together pick one of the groups' ideas to discuss further. Then ask:

- Now imagine that God is the producer for this particular 5-minute movie.
- What changes might God make? What new ideas might God contribute? What other touches might God add?
- In general, what do you imagine God thinks about the current state of entertainment?

TaLK SHoW MaNiA

Recruit four volunteers, one to play *a talk-show host* and the other three to play *God, a television* and *a typical TV viewer*. Ask the volunteers to sit in chairs in the center of the group. Offer these directions:

- The *host* leads a discussion about television, allowing the guests to speak from their roles about the power and use or misuse of television.
- *God* might says things like, "TV, when it's good, can be very good. In fact, I have my favorite shows..."
- *The television* might say things like, "Come on, what's all the fuss...don't I offer you great entertainment? I'm your friend! Trust me."
- *The TV viewer* might say things like, "Sometimes it's so confusing   so many choices...so little time."

Let the volunteers continue the talk-show for 5-10 minutes, then repeat with other volunteers if members seem interested. Ask:

- What new ideas did we hear about television in our TV talk show?
- What insights have you gained today about your own TV habits?

21

WHaT'S yOUR OPiNioN?

Invite group members to respond freely to these statements about modern media:

- Movies, music videos, video games and television encourage disrespect, violence and immorality in our culture.
- Movies, music videos, video games and television simply reflect the truth about our culture.
- People who don't like today's media simply should not watch and listen.
- People learn about life from today's media.
- Parents should be able to control what their teenagers watch and listen to.
- I've learned a lot about good and evil, right and wrong from TV, movies and magazines.

THe MOVie I WoULD mAKE

Invite volunteers to brainstorm the movies they've always wanted to make:

- What, in brief, would be the plot of your movie?
- Who would star in your movie?
- What message would your movie have?
- How would people be affected by seeing your movie?
- Why would people want to see your movie? What would make your movie stand out? In what ways would it be unlike any movie previously made?

WHo AM I SuPPoSED TO Be?

Distribute **two large pieces of poster board, a pair of scissors** and **an assortment of recent magazines geared for youth and/or dealing with fashion and fitness**. Invite group members to put together two posters, using cut- or torn-out photos and words, one illustrating how a young woman is "supposed" to look, think, feel and act and the other illustrating how a young man is "supposed" to look, think, feel and act. Let the posters reflect contemporary standards and values, both of appearance and accomplishment.

After the posters are completed, discuss:

- How do the teenagers whom you know compare to this media image?
- What pressures do such media images place on today's teenagers? What is the result?
- What percentage of today's teenagers accept the media image of the "ideal" young person?
- What percentage of today's teenagers believe that they meet the media image of the "ideal" young person?

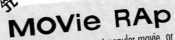

THe aWARdS SHOW

Explore group members' movie-going tastes and habits with a mock "Academy Awards." Begin by inviting members to propose a variety of categories; encourage them to include categories beyond the obvious ones of "best picture," "best actor," "best actress," etc., for example:

- best action sequence
- dumbest plot
- funniest line
- greatest special effects
- most boring romantic scene

Let group members nominate their favorites, then vote to determine the winners.

MOViE RAp

Together attend a current popular movie, or rent and view a recent **movie** now on video.

After viewing the movie, discuss:

- What did you like about the movie? What worked for you?
- What didn't you like about the movie? What did you think was unbelievable or phony?
- Every movie has a message. What do you think this movie was saying? What did the movie's producer and director want you to believe? to do? to think? to feel?
- How did this movie use these elements to get its message across:
  — music
  — lighting
  — action
  — dialogue
  — editing (how the bits and pieces of film are assembled into smoothly flowing action)
  — sound
  — special effects
  — suspense
  — humor

- If you had produced or directed this movie, what would you have done differently?
- If God had produced or directed this movie, what do you imagine God might have done differently?

WHaT'S NorMAL?

Distribute **paper** and **pencils** with this explanation: We just arrived from another planet. We want to study the "normal" teenager on Earth. To make the most efficient use of our time, we will divide into five groups, each of which will take a look at a different event or item related to teen life to get a clear picture of what it means to be a teenager today.

Divide participants into five groups. Ask each group to discuss one of these events or items, summarizing on paper what this event or item tells them about today's teenagers, using no other information than what they can glean from their assigned event or item:

■ a junior high or high school math class
■ several currently popular TV shows starring teenagers
■ 3 hours of MTV
■ a copy of a teen-oriented magazine
■ a church group similar to ours

Each group can ask, concerning its area:

■ From what we observe here and now in this setting (or item), what do we learn about today's teens?
— What do they value?
— What do they want out of life?
— What do they think and feel?
— How do they treat others?
— What do they talk about?
— How do they feel about themselves?

Give groups time to discuss, then gather and ask groups to report.

RaTinG YOuR LIFe

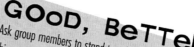

Ask group members to use the movie rating system to rate various areas of their lives:

G   General Audiences
PG   Parental Guidance Suggested
PG-13   Parent Caution
R   Restricted
NC-17   No Children Under 17 Allowed

Using the above rating system, how would you rate:

- your television viewing?
- your movie viewing?
- your music listening?
- your magazine reading?
- your book reading?
- your video-game playing?

You could also invite group members to use the same rating system to rate:

- their home life
- their love life
- their thought life
- their school life
- their friendships
- their spiritual life

GOOD, BeTTeR, BeST

Ask group members to stand together in a circle. Invite each group member to complete this statement:

- This week, each time I want to watch TV I'll consider...

Close by praying:

- Dear God of what's good, help us to reflect you in the choices we make this week when it comes to television. Amen.

TV EX-CoMMiTMeNT

Distribute **index cards** and **pens**. Invite group members to finish this sentence:

- This week, I'll give up an hour of TV, specifically (name a program) so that I can...

Suggest that they put their index cards on a mirror to remind them through the week.

BeHiND THe HYpE

Divide participants into smaller groups of 4-5 members each. Distribute **paper** and **pencils**. Ask all groups to design and draw a magazine or newspaper advertisement for a new soft drink that tastes like pineapple. Each group chooses its own name for the drink, then designs its ad. Groups may want to keep in mind:

■ what benefits the drink offers
■ why it's better than any other soft drink
■ what "mood" or "attitude" they want people to associate with the drink

The assignment for groups differs only in this respect: the age of those to whom they are trying to sell. One group designs the ad to appeal to small children, one to elementary-age children, one to teenagers, one to young adults, one to middle-aged adults and one to older adults.

After the ads have been completed, ask groups to show and explain them to the other groups. Discuss:

■ Which of our ads seem particularly effective? Why?
■ How did our approaches to the ads differ for the different age groups?
■ In what ways do our ads exaggerate or twist the truth?
■ What have we learned about advertising from this activity?
■ In what ways can we keep ourselves from being fooled by the exaggerated claims or subtle associations in contemporary advertising?

WHaT'S IN? WHaT'S OUT?

Prepare **two sheets of poster board,** one labeled *What's In?* and the other *What's Out?*

Ask group members to suggest TV shows, movie stars, musicians, hairstyles, clothing styles, celebrities, foods—whatever—that are currently both "in" and "out." List these on the appropriate sheets of poster board. Expect some disagreement. Let group members debate these disputed suggestions. After a dozen or more items have been listed on each poster, discuss:

- Which of our "out" items were once "in"? Which "in" items were once considered "out"?
- What determines whether something is "in" or "out"?
- To what extent is what is "in" or "out" determined by the media (television, movies, music videos, magazines, advertising, etc.)? by our friends? by our own choices?
- In what ways can following (or *not following*) what is "in" or "out" unite us with people? separate us from people?
- In what ways can following (or *not following*) what is "in" or "out" help us accept ourselves? *not accept ourselves?*
- In what ways can following (or *not following*) what is "in" or "out" bring us closer to God? keep us from God?

Poverty & Wealth

POVERTY &
WEALTH

GReED OR GOoDNeSS

Invite participants to discuss:

■ Define *materialism*. (Record suggestions on **chalkboard or newsprint**.)

■ Do you think that the accumulation of wealth and possessions is bad? Why?

■ Describe a materialistic person.

■ What contributes to materialism? (*Examples*: parents, advertising, peer pressure, personal choice)

■ Rate yourself on a scale of 1 (not at all) to 10 (very) on how materialistic you are. Would you change your rating if you could? What would you expect to gain from being more or less materialistic?

CoMMeRCiAL HyPe

Distribute **paper** and **pencils**. Invite each group member to make a list of things he or she would like to receive at Christmas or on a birthday this year. Share these lists with each other and discuss:

■ What are the most important items on our lists? Which items bring joy?

■ How have our lists changed as we have grown older?

■ Define *commercialism*. Give examples of commercialism.

■ In what ways do advertisements shape our expectations of what life should be?

■ What can we do to cope with commercialism?

CoNSuMeRiSM: PERSuASiVE PoVeRTY

Before your meeting ask several group members to help you gather **examples of teen-oriented advertising**. Possibilities include print advertisements from teen magazines, video-taped television advertisements from shows popular with teens and video-taped portions of music videos.

One by one, display the examples, asking after each:

■ To whom is this ad targeted? How do you know?

■ How do you respond to this ad? to the models? the colors? the music? the sets? the clothes? the editing?

■ What is the mood of the ad? the feel?

■ The people who produced this ad want you to believe something about yourself, about life, about your needs or about your worth. What do they want you to believe? Is it true? Do you believe it?

■ The people who produced this ad want you to do something. What is it? Will you do it? Why or why not?

■ Many ads work at the level of association. We learn nothing about the product, but we associate the product with feeling strong, looking sexy or being cool. To what degree is this ad an ad of association?

■ Overall, is this ad honest? affirming? insulting? effective? loving?

POVeRTY AND PROSTiTUTiON

Discuss:
- Define *prostitution*. (Consult a **dictionary** for help.)
- Share your thoughts and feelings about prostitution.
- What feelings, life experiences and values do you think contribute to a person becoming a prostitute? using a prostitute?
- What does Paul say about prostitution in 1 Corinthians 6:15-20?
- How do you think Christians should respond to prostitution? to users of prostitution? to the prostitutes themselves?
- How does prostitution stem from poverty? lead to poverty?

RE-aCT-iON

Invite group members to share about situations of economic inequality they have experienced or witnessed. They may wish to tell about seeing a family begging on the street or about their own feelings of inferiority at the affluence of others. Encourage them to talk about the feelings attached to the experience. After each member has had a chance to tell his or her story, let the group discuss:

- What action could be taken in that situation?

RuNNiNG AWaY

Before the session ask a group member to serve as leader of this discussion. Together with the member-leader, contact local or state agencies that provide emergency services to runaways and ask them for **information**. One national resource is the National Hotline for Runaways: 1-800-621-4000.

Encourage the member-leader to choose and plan an activity to lead into the discussion. Suggestions:
- Complete this sentence: *If I ever ran away, it would be because...*
- Debate the pros and cons of running away to escape an abusive home situation.

- Combine drawings, magazine headlines, photographs and written phrases to make a collage depicting life on the street.

Prepare with the member-leader a list of discussion questions, for example:
- Why might teenagers run away today?
- Share a story about someone who ran away.
- How can we help someone who is talking about running away?

In the session take a "back seat" as the member-leader leads.

GaMBLiNG: RiCHeS OR PoVeRTY?

Explain that you are going to experiment with gambling. Distribute **play money, bingo cards** and **bingo tokens** to each group member. Provide a *small* amount of money ($200-300) to some members and a *large* amount of money ($2,000-4,000) to others. Each bingo card costs $100, and players may buy and play as many cards as they wish or can afford. Play the game. For each round, the first person to complete bingo wins all the cash paid for that round.

WiTHOuT A HoME

Before your meeting contact a local shelter or social service agency to get **current statistics on the homeless near your community**. The shelter or agency may provide speakers (including members of your community's homeless population) to meet and talk with your group.

Share the information you have gathered. Ask:
■ Imagine life without a home. If you were homeless in your town or city, what would you miss most? Where would you look for food? for warmth on cold nights?

for clothes when yours wore out? for friendship when you felt lonely? for medical care when you were sick?
■ What is your personal reaction to homeless people?
■ Why do we sometimes fear homeless people? What are we reminded of when we see homeless people?

Plan and carry out a project to help relieve the suffering of the homeless in your area. A local shelter or food pantry may have projects you could help with, or organize your own collection and distribution program for food or clothes.

Play at least six rounds before discussing:
■ Who is "broke"? Who is "wealthy"?
  ■ In what way are we "gambling"? What difference would real money make?
  ■ If you won money, how did you feel? How did winning affect your desire to play again?
  ■ If you only lost money, how did you feel? How did losing affect your desire to continue playing?
■ Imagine that the play money represented our actual wealth. Who took the biggest "gamble," the wealthy or the poor? Explain. Who risked their shelter, food and clothing, the wealthy or the poor? Explain.
■ Consider God's role in gambling. How does our bingo game demonstrate trust in God? in self? in "chance"? in money? How is God involved when we play the lottery? when we feed slot machines? when we bet on sports events?

FOoD FoR aLL?

Before the meeting set up three tables, one with **snacks**, one with **rice** and one with **food scraps**. Bring **adhesive name tags,** for each participant. Write a large #1 on 1/3 of the tags, a #2 on another third, and a #3 on the last third.

In the meeting, distribute the numbered tags. Instruct the #1s to gather around the snack table, #2s around the rice table and #3s around the garbage table. Invite group members to eat from their tables. Do not allow them to share food. After a few moments of this, continue with the activity Less Means More (p. 34).

HuNGER iS...

Distribute **Bibles** and ask volunteers to read aloud Proverbs 25:21, Isaiah 58:7-10 and Ezekiel 18:5, 7. Divide into three groups and assign each group one of the three scriptures. Give these instructions: Create a short skit based on your assigned scripture. Let it communicate whatever truth about hunger that you find. The skit may be set in any historical time period or situation.

After several minutes of preparation, let each group present its skit. Ask:
- What did each skit say about hunger? About responsibility?
- What did the skits have in common?
- How were the skits relevant to our own experience?

ReAL HoMeLeSSNeSS

Divide into groups of three. Give these instructions: Imagine that all three of you have been kicked out of your homes and have no one to take you in. All you have is each other. What do you do? Where do you go? What do you feel? How will you protect yourselves? Tell us a story about your experience on the streets.

After 10 minutes of preparation, let each group tell its story of homelessness. Then ask:
- What dangers do teens uniquely face when dealing with homelessness?

DROPPiNG OuT: A STeP iNTO POVeRTY?

Before your meeting invite **two guest speakers** to join you for your discussion. The first guest could represent the advantages of staying in school — perhaps a high school teacher or an employer. The second guest could represent the position that dropping out may be right for some students, for example, someone who had built a successful business without the benefit of a high school diploma.

Invite both guests to present their positions and respond to group members' questions. Then ask:

- Who has seriously considered dropping out? What looked like the advantages? disadvantages?
- If anyone has dropped out, what have been the consequences, both positive and negative?
- What makes the typical high school "system" work for some students and not for others?
- What could we do to make the system work for more students?

WHy aM I HeRE?

Distribute **pencils** and **paper** and divide participants into small groups of 3-4 members each. Ask groups to discuss the questions below:

- Think of a typical teenager. What does that teenager live for? If asked the question, "Why are you here?", what do you think he or she would say?
- What do we live for? What is our ultimate goal?
- If you could ask God, "What are we here for?", how do you think God would answer?

When groups have finished, invite groups to share the highlights of their discussions. Continue:

- What is *hedonism?* (the pursuit of pleasure as the highest goal in life)
- How hedonistic is our culture? the typical teenager? the typical adult?
- What alternative "life-goals," other than hedonism, can we identify? (Invite a volunteer to list ideas on **chalkboard or newsprint**; include hedonism in the list.)
- How do our life-goals affect our day-to-day decisions and choices? the way we treat others? our relationship to God?
- Finish this sentence: The ultimate goal of my life is...

HuNGeR iN A WoRLD OF PLeNTY

Before your meeting request **resources on world hunger** from one of the following agencies:

Bread for the World
1100 Wayne Avenue, Suite 1000
Silver Spring, MD 20910
(301) 608-2400

Oxfam America
26 West Street
Boston, MA 02111-1206
(617) 482-1211

Discuss:

■ What might it feel like to be truly hungry? How might severe hunger affect out bodies? our minds? our attitudes toward others? our ability to care for others?

■ What knowledge do we have of world hunger? of its causes?

■ What knowledge do we have of hunger in our own community? of its causes?

■ What responsibility do Christians have in the face of world hunger?

■ What can we do about hunger in our community?

Consider organizing a project to help fight hunger in your community. Suggestions include helping out at a soup kitchen or collecting food for a food pantry.

LeSS MEaNS MoRE

Begin with the activity Food for All? (p. 32). Then divide into small groups, making sure that each group contains a mixture of #1s, #2s and #3s. Let each group member talk about his or her experience of privilege or poverty from the preceding activity. Also ask each group member to speak about how he or she reacted to the experiences of the others.

After group members have debriefed, gather again to discuss:

■ What did we learn from each other?
■ What are the responsibilities or advantages of having more or less food than you have now?

34

THe VaLuE OF HeDONiSM

Distribute to each group member an equal amount of **play money**. Spread out on a table the following objects: assorted **items of value** (e.g., Bible, car keys, cash, portable CD player), **pictures of items of value** (e.g., family, groceries, home theater system, video game system, perfect body, etc.), and **index cards** on each of which is written one word identifying an intangible item of value, for example: *faith, happiness, self-esteem, acceptance, fame, love,* etc. Let group members look through these.

Then conduct an auction:

- Hold up one item, picture or index card. Identify what is being auctioned.
- Invite group members to bid on the item.
- Collect the amount bid from the highest bidder and let him or her have the item, picture or index card.
- Continue with the next item.

When all items have been sold or all the money spent, stop and discuss:

- How did you decide what to purchase?
- To what degree do your purchases reflect your real-life values and goals?

RiCH vs. PooR

Invite several members of your church's or community's social action groups to prepare a **brief presentation on poverty in your community.** Ask speakers to include a description of ways the social action groups are currently responding to these needs. Allow time for group members' questions.

Ask group members to brainstorm ways they would like to help meet community needs. They may want to participate in an ongoing project, such as helping in a community soup kitchen, or initiate a new project, such as taking sandwiches to people living on the street.

Help the group members to decide:

- what group members will do
- how each group member can be involved
- how group members will ensure a follow-through on their plans

HeDONiSM OR HEaVeN

Distribute **Bibles** and invite group members to turn together to Daniel 1:3-16. Ask a volunteer to read this passage aloud. After the reading, discuss:

- Why are Daniel and his friends chosen for the royal court?
- What problem does this pose for Daniel? (See v. 8.)
- What deal does Daniel cut with Ashpenaz?
- What's the result for Daniel and his friends?
- Daniel made a choice between following God's will and enjoying the pleasures of the king's court...between God and hedonism. When do we face similar choices?
- What enables us, like Daniel, to choose God?

Optional question for further discussion:
Some people talk about "holy hedonism." Holy hedonism suggests that anytime we choose what is right and holy, we automatically choose what's best for ourselves as well, and what is most pleasurable in the long run. What do you think?

BaLANCiNG PLeASuRE

Divide the **chalkboard or newsprint** into two columns. Label one column *Serving Others* and the other *Having Fun*. Number 1 to 10 in both columns. Explain that having fun is important and serving others is important. *Finding the balance is the challenge.* Ask group members to suggest ways that they have found to serve God and ways that they have found to have fun...*that are compatible with each other.*

As group members make suggestions, have a volunteer record responses in the appropriate columns. Stop when 10 items have been listed in each column.

ENTeRTAiNMeNT ...ENOuGH!

Distribute **Bibles, paper** and **pencils**. Divide participants into three groups and assign each group a portion of scripture:

- Ecclesiastes 2:1-3
- Ecclesiastes 2:4-8
- Ecclesiastes 2:9-11

Offer these instructions: With the members of your group, read your assigned scripture. After the reading, rewrite your portion of the scripture in contemporary terms, appropriate for today's teenagers. For example, if your group is working on verses 1-3, what "good times" might the philosopher (the author of Ecclesiastes) pursue as a modern-day teenager? If your group is working on verses 4-8, what "great things" might the philosopher pursue in the search for meaning? If your group is working on verses 9-11, what might a teenager say instead of "I was great"? perhaps "I was popular"? "I was the perfect teen"?

Give groups about 10 minutes to finish their rewriting of the scripture, then regather and ask groups, in order, to read aloud their new versions of Ecclesiastes 2:1-11. Then ask:

- To what extent do you think the philosopher was addicted to entertainment? to accomplishment?
- To what extent do you share the philosopher's view of life?
- What role does God play in the philosopher's view of life?

HoMeLeSSNeSS: REaL SOLuTiONS?

Post a sheet of **newsprint** on the wall. Divide it into five columns, labeling them *Causes, Families, Churches, Government* and *Schools.* Brainstorm causes of homelessness and list these in the first column. Then begin with each cause listed and proceed across your chart with each column, asking how that group in each case can both prevent homelessness and help homeless people.

Violence

VIOLENCE

FaMiLY HONoR

Distribute **Bibles** and ask a volunteer to read aloud Ephesians 5:21. Ask:

■ What do you think it means "to submit" to one another in your family?

■ What are some healthy ways to submit? What are some unhealthy ways to submit?

■ In what ways is this verse or its concept used to justify domestic violence?

■ How might mutual submission in a family help prevent or eliminate violence?

Then ask another volunteer to read aloud Ephesians 6:1-4. Ask:

■ Imagine that we are all parents of teenage children. Someone visits our group to ask us about parenting. How would you answer these questions:

— What's the toughest part of parenting a teenager?

— When do you feel angry at your teenager? How do you handle anger?

— What do you do to keep your family violence-free?

— What makes your teenager angry? Why?

— What do you think is the best way to give your children "Christian discipline and instruction"?

i REMeMBER WHeN...

Ask group members to spend a few moments recalling a true-life example of family violence, either from their own family, from the news or from a friend's experience. Then invite volunteers to tell their stories, describing each of the characters involved and the factors that led to the abuse.

Note: Those in your group who have experienced violence in the home may not wish to share. Give permission to everyone to pass on the storytelling or to couch the story in the third-person.

When those who wish to tell stories have done so, discuss:

■ What can we say about the causes of family violence?

■ What do you think needs to be done to stop family violence?

■ What some people call abuse in the family another person might call discipline. When does discipline cross the line into abuse?

FaMiLY ViOLeNCE: 3 STRaTEGiES

On a large sheet of **newsprint**, make three columns. Label them *Parent/Parent*, *Parent/Child* and *Child/Child*. Talk about abuse involving each of these pairs of family members and invite group members to brainstorm different ways to cope in each situation. Help the group to include:

■ ideas on what the victim could do to protect him- or herself

■ ideas on how someone outside the situation could get help for the victim

■ ideas on how to stop the abuser

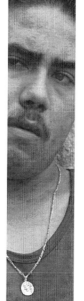

PUNiSHMeNT: NO CLEaR ANSWeRS

Distribute **Bibles** and ask group members to read silently Romans 12:17–13:5. As they read, make two columns on **chalkboard or newsprint**. Label one *Supports Capital Punishment* and the other *Opposes Capital Punishment*. Then invite group members to call out ways they think the passage supports and/or opposes capital punishment. Record ideas in the appropriate columns. Then ask:

■ What do you think Paul's primary concern is in 12:17-21? in 13:1-5? How do these ideas cooperate?

■ What is the difference as Paul sees it between punishment and revenge?

BULLiES

Write the word *Bully* on **chalkboard or newsprint**. Ask group members to brainstorm characteristics of bullies as a volunteer lists their suggestions. Discuss:

■ Why do people bully others?

■ What feelings do you think bullies have?

■ What do bullies hope to get out of bullying others?

■ What is different between the way gals bully and the way guys bully? (*Studies suggest that girls tend to bully psychologically while boys tend to bully physically.*)

■ How are bullies different in high school than they were in junior high or middle school? than in elementary school?

■ Who do you think might be the bullies in your parents' world?

CHiLD ABuSE ...NeVER

Invite a **speaker** from your city or county social services department or a child-abuse prevention and assistance program to present a short talk on child abuse to the group. Ask the speaker also to bring written information for group members.

Encourage questions at the conclusion of the talk. You may wish to ask the speaker to respond to the following questions:

■ What, in general, can today's teenagers do to fight child abuse?

■ What, specifically, should we do if we knows that someone (a sibling, relative, friend, etc.) is currently being abused?

■ What can teenagers do if they feel that they have been emotionally, physically or sexually abused in the past?

■ What can we do if we feel we are being abused *now?*

SEXUAL ABUSE FACTS

Sexual abuse experts estimate that 1 out of every 3 females and 1 out of every 4 males will be sexually abused by the age of 18. Sexual abuse cuts across ethnic, socioeconomic and religious boundaries. Therefore, sexual abuse is likely to be a reality in the lives of several members of your group. The emotional, physical, mental and spiritual scars of sexual abuse last into adulthood, affecting self-esteem and the ability to relate to others.

MaRKETiNG ViOLENCE

Begin with the activity Horror Snippets (p. 43). Then ask:

- How did you feel as you watched the opening clips? thrilled? excited? disgusted? angry? upset?
- What do you think was the purpose behind each example of violence?
- Do you think violence on TV is a problem? Explain.
- When might TV violence be justified? For example, when might TV violence motivate us? inform us? help us?
- When is the violence on TV unnecessary? How could we distinguish between necessary and unnecessary violence? Why does violence on TV sell? What attracts us to violence?

SeXuAL ABuSE

Before tackling this topic, **get the facts**. Contact organizations that specialize in child abuse, for example: the National Center for Missing and Exploited Children, 2101 Wilson Blvd., Ste. 550, Arlington, VA 22201 or the Kempe National Center for the Prevention and Treatment of Child Abuse, 1205 Oneida, Denver, CO 80220. Ask for information specifically written for high school teens. Be aware that you may be ethically and legally bound to report disturbing information heard in this discussion.

Review the information gathered **before the session** and invite group members to share their views and feelings about sexual abuse. Discuss:

- How aware are you of sexual abuse among your friends and classmates?
- What is our responsibility if we know of sexual abuse in our families or among our friends?
- To whom would you go if you knew about or suspected sexual abuse? What would you risk by telling? by *not* telling?
- What would we want to say to someone who has been or is being sexually abused? to the sexual abuser?
- Respond to these statements about sexual abuse, expressing agreement or disagreement and explaining why:
  - Sexual abuse is a problem in many families—even in "happy" families.
  - Sexual abuse is a crime and a sign that something is wrong with the abuser.
  - No one deserves to be sexually abused; it is not the fault of the abused.
  - Your body is yours and a gift from God. You have a right to say no, angrily.
  - Healthy families do not keep secrets. If you are sexually abused, tell someone!
  - Sexual abuse angers God. If you are abused, God is on your side.

WaR UNENDiNG

Ask:

■ On a scale of 1 (low) to 10 (high), how likely do you think it is that you will experience war firsthand in your lifetime? Explain your ranking.

■ What do you think causes war? Do you think war is sometimes necessary? Why or why not?

■ How would people need to change for war to stop? How would Christians need to change?

■ What are realistic ways Christians can work for peace? What are realistic ways Christians can rely on God's power instead of the power of violence?

CAiN OR CHRiST

Distribute **Bibles** and invite five volunteers to read dramatically Genesis 4:1-16, assigning these parts: narrator, Eve, Cain and the Lord. Before the reading, explain that this story features the first act of violence recorded in the Bible. As you listen to the reading, try to identify the source of the violence.

Invite the volunteers to present their reading, then discuss:

■ Why does Cain kill his brother? What was Cain feeling? Why?

■ To what extent is the source of Cain's violence the source of all violence?

■ What is the result of Cain's act of violence?

■ To what extent is this result also the result of today's violence?

Ask a volunteer to read aloud 2 Corinthians 5:17-21 as other group members follow along. Discuss: While Genesis 4 talks of the source of violence, St. Paul describes the cure for violence. What

■ While Genesis 4 talks of the source of violence, St. Paul describes the cure for violence. What provision has God made for sin and violence?

■ How does one take part in God's cure for violence?

Questions for deeper discussion:

■ What does this comparison of Cain and Christ say about the possibilities for our families?

■ How could God's cure for violence change today's battles between rival gangs? the physical and sexual abuse of children? hate crimes against Jews, African-Americans, gays and other targeted groups?

HoRROR SNiPPeTS

Before the meeting, videotape examples of television violence. Keep segments to 30 seconds or less and include clips from a variety of shows, including the evening news, so-called "reality shows" (like Rescue 911), sports, MTV music videos, television dramas and cartoons. In your meeting room, prepare the **television, VCR** and **tape** for viewing.

Identify one wall of the meeting space as the *Very Violent Wall* and the opposite wall as the *Not Very Violent Wall*. Give these instructions: I'm going to show a clip from something on television this past week. If you think this clip is very violent, move immediately to the *Very Violent Wall*. If you think the clip wasn't really violent, move immediately to the *Not Very Violent Wall*. You may stand anywhere between the two walls to reflect your exact opinion.

Show the first clip, stop the VCR and ask group members to move quickly to either wall (or to any space in between). When they have moved, ask them to look around them to see where others are standing. After each clip, ask one or two group members to explain their position between the two walls. You might also invite any two people whose positions differ widely to debate their opinions. Repeat for all the clips, then continue with the activity Marketing Violence (p. 41) or another discussion about television violence.

A PRaYER FOR PeaCE

Copy the Prayer of St. Francis on **chalkboard or newsprint**. Explain that it was written over 700 years ago, but that the human issues are the same. Pray it aloud in unison.

> Lord, make us instruments of your peace. Where there is hatred, let us sow love; where there is injury, pardon; where there is discord, union; where there is doubt, faith; where there is despair, hope; where there is darkness, light; where there is sadness, joy. Grant that we may not so much seek to be consoled as to console; to be understood as to understand; to be loved as to love. For it is in giving that we receive; it is in pardoning that we are pardoned; and it is in dying that we are born to eternal life. *Amen.*

GuNS WHy?

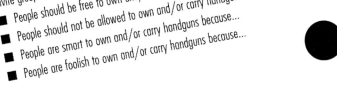

Invite group members to complete one or all of these sentences:

- People should be free to own and/or carry handguns because...
- People should not be allowed to own and/or carry handguns because..
- People are smart to own and/or carry handguns because...
- People are foolish to own and/or carry handguns because...

THe GuN DEBaTE

Set up a **table** with **two chairs** in the front of the room. Ask group members who are against handgun control to sit on one side of the room, and those who identify themselves as for handgun control to sit on the opposite side of the room. Explain to group members that they are going to debate the issue of gun control. They are free to question and dispute each others' ideas. They are *not* free to attack people or their character.

Have a member of each team sit in one of the chairs. The pro-control person has 1 minute to make a statement supporting his or her beliefs. Then the anti-control person has 1 minute to respond.

Whenever a group member finishes a statement, another member of his or her team may step forward and "tag" the teammate out of the chair.

Tagged members return to their groups, and tagging members take their places. Always alternate speakers from team to team. Continue while interest is sustained. Then ask:

- What are the best arguments we heard on both sides?
- What do both sides have in common?
- What suggestions for reducing handgun violence did we hear from both sides?
- Has anyone changed their views on gun control? Why?

Note: Undoubtedly the debate will include reference to the Second Amendment to the U.S. Constitution, which reads: A well-regulated militia being necessary to the security of a free State, the right of the people to keep and bear arms shall not be infringed.

KiLLiNG EaCH OTHeR

Invite group members to respond to these 1993 statistics:

- Each day, 160,000 U.S. students skip school because they are afraid of violence.
- 100,000 U.S. kids carry guns to school. 700,000 carry knives.
- Every day in the U.S., 14,000 students and 40 teachers are attacked.

Then ask:

- Would you own a handgun? Why or why not?
- In what ways has violence with guns affected you personally?
- What limits on handgun ownership do you think are reasonable? Why?

CaPiTAL PuNiSHMeNT

Before your meeting prepare **two index cards** per participant. Each participant should receive one card that says "I AGREE" and one card that says "I DISAGREE."

Distribute the response cards and ask group members to hold up a card in response to the following statements. Add other statements of your own:

- Death is a fitting punishment for murder.
- Capital punishment is another form of murder.
- Death is a fitting punishment for rape.
- Killing someone, even a criminal, is never appropriate.
- Death is appropriate for child molesters.
- I could personally throw the switch for an execution.
- There are cases in which capital punishment is appropriate.

Ask group members to discuss their reactions to any of the statements. Ask:

- When is the taking of life wrong? right?
- How do you think God feels about capital punishment?
- In what ways do God's generosity and capital punishment relate?

CRiME aND PUNiSHMeNT

Set up the meeting space like a courtroom with a judge's bench, jury box and defendant's chair. Recruit a volunteer to play the first judge for this activity. Have the judge choose six group members to be the first jury. The jury takes its place and the judge explains that the first defendant has been tried and found guilty. You or a volunteer may serve as the clerk of the court and read the charges of the first defendant as described below, embellishing both the description of the defendant and the crime.

The judge then gives the jury 3 minutes to decide on an appropriate punishment for the defendant. When the time is up, the judge calls for the jury's decision. A representative of the jury stands and announces its decision. Repeat the activity for the remaining defendants on the list. For each defendant, recruit a new judge and new jury members.

Defendants/Crimes:

- Jenny: 7-year-old female who took three cookies from her grandparent's cookie jar without permission
- Daryl: 18-year-old male whose neglect led to the accidental death by drowning of a 3-year-old boy he was babysitting
- Bianca: 29-year-old female whose drunk driving resulted in the death of a mother and her two children
- Randy: 41-year-old male who fatally stabbed another man in an argument over drugs
- Ken: 53-year-old male who raped an 18-year-old female

HoW TO DECiDE

Begin with the activity Crime and Punishment (previous column). After all punishments have been determined, discuss:

- What guided our choice of punishments?
- On what did jury members disagree?
- Overall, do you think the punishments chosen by our juries were harsh? lenient? fair? unfair?
- What's the purpose of punishment?
- What different principles could be used in determining a punishment, for example:
  — eye for an eye (vengeance)
  — change the heart (rehabilitation)
  — protect the rest of us
  — make an example for society

A WaRRiOR WiTHOuT WeAPoNS

Distribute **Bibles** and recruit three volunteers to read aloud 1 Samuel 17:41-51, each taking one part: David, Goliath, narrator.

Then ask group members to retell the story in contemporary terms: setting, weapons, enemies, issues at stake, etc. Ask:

- God plays an important role in David's story. What does God do in our story?
- What might our story suggest about today's problems with weapons and violence?

CAPiTAL PUNiSHMeNT: PRo aND CoN

Before your meeting clip and make **copies of accounts of heinous crimes or trials** reported in local or national newspapers. Begin by asking:

- What is capital punishment? *(penalty of death for a crime)*

Then distribute the copies of news articles and ask group members to read them silently. When they have finished reading, invite members to choose a side in the issue:

- In general, without doing any additional discussing, which side of this issue do you tend to support? Are you, in general, for or against capital punishment?

Ask those who support capital punishment to gather on one side of the room and those who oppose capital punishment to gather on the opposite side of the room. Stage a debate, allowing representatives from each side to give 30-second statements in support of their positions. Alternate statements from side to side. After about 10 minutes, ask groups to physically switch sides of the room. Explain:

- You now are on the *other* side of the debate, representing the side you just opposed. No matter what you actually believe, it's your job to support the opposite opinion.

After another 10 minutes, stop and discuss:

- What new ideas about capital punishment have you heard in this debate?
- How have your beliefs about capital punishment changed through this activity?